SECOND YEAR ASSESSMENT PAPERS IN

ENGLISH

ANSWER BOOK

J M BOND

Nelson

Paper 1

Underline the right answers.

Mr. and Mrs. Bingham are sheep farmers in Australia. They own a large sheep station at Woomero, where they have divided their land into several big fields, called paddocks. One paddock may be larger than a whole farm in Britain. The sheep must not be allowed to stray, so there are fences all round each paddock. These also stop wild dogs, called dingoes, getting in to the sheep and killing them.

1. The wild dogs are (paddocks, <u>dingoes,</u> Woomero)

2. The fields are called (sheep stations, <u>paddocks,</u> fences)

3. Where do Mr. and Mrs. Bingham live?
   (Dingo, England, <u>Woomero)</u>

4. How do they stop the sheep straying?
   (They are guarded by dogs, put in sheds, <u>fenced in)</u>

5. What would a dingo try to do to the sheep?
   (<u>Kill them,</u> let them out, go wild)

6. A British farm may be (larger than a sheep station, smaller than a train, <u>smaller than a paddock)</u>

Fill in the gaps.

7. T ....<u>ues</u>.... day is the day before Wednesday.

8. There are sixty minutes in an h ....<u>our</u>....

9. We have eight fingers and two th ....<u>umbs</u>....

10. I am drying my hands on the to ....<u>wel</u>....

11. I put the cup and s ....<u>auc</u>.... er on the table.

12. He gave the book to his fr ....<u>iend</u>....

Arrange these words in the order in which you would find them in the dictionary.

colour   dark   elephant   danger   egg   change

13 (1) __change__   14 (2) __colour__   15 (3) __danger__

16 (4) __dark__   17 (5) __egg__   18 (6) __elephant__

Underline the word which does not fit in with the rest.

19 leg   ankle   knee   arm   <u>gloves</u>

20 March   May   November   <u>Monday</u>   April

21 <u>say</u>   happy   glad   pleased   cheerful

22 whistle   sing   shout   scream   <u>silence</u>

23 write   <u>sleep</u>   draw   crayon   paint

Write the plural of these words.

24 box   __boxes__   25 man   __men__   26 child   __children__

27 foot   __feet__   28 baby   __babies__

Underline the word which rhymes with the first word in each line.

29 **sail**   call   sill   <u>pale</u>   fall   well

30 **won**   ten   gone   bin   <u>done</u>   tone

31 **eight**   later   might   sight   bite   <u>hate</u>

32 **knot**   know   <u>pot</u>   note   boat   goat

33 **die**   may   see   lay   bee   <u>high</u>

Put a question mark **?** or an exclamation mark **!** in the right place in the following sentences.

34 "Where is your book?" said the teacher.

35 The girl said, "Please will you help me?"

36 Mr. Brown said, "Sit down at once!"

3

Underline the right word in the brackets.

37 Mum said, "You must (rap, <u>wrap)</u> the scarf round your neck. It is very cold."

38 I heard the carol singers (<u>rap,</u> wrap) on the door.

39 Dad said, "Go out for a walk so I can have some (piece, <u>peace).</u>

40 Auntie Jan told him that he might have a (<u>piece,</u> peace) of cake.

Paper 2

Underline the right answers.

There was an old woman who swallowed a cow;
I don't know how
She swallowed a cow;
She swallowed the cow to catch the dog,
She swallowed the dog to catch the cat,
She swallowed the cat to catch the bird,
She swallowed the bird to catch the spider,
That wriggled and jiggled and tickled inside her.
She swallowed the spider to catch the fly,
I don't know why
She swallowed the fly.
Perhaps she'll die.

There was an old woman who swallowed a horse;
She died, of course!

4

1 She swallowed (1, 3, 7, 8) animals.

2 Why did she swallow the spider? (To catch the fly, to catch the bird, to catch the cow)

3 Which animal was swallowed first? (The fly, the spider, the horse)

4 Which animal was swallowed last? (The fly, the spider, the horse)

5 What happened when she swallowed the horse? (She swallowed the cow, she died, she wriggled)

6 Is this story true? (Yes, no, I don't know)

Underline the word with an opposite meaning from the word on the left.

7	**give**	take	present	have	pass
8	**hard**	uncomfortable	difficult	work	soft
9	**quick**	fast	slow	run	rush
10	**begin**	began	start	enter	finish
11	**bright**	clever	dull	shining	polish
12	**top**	spin	above	bottom	high

Put these sentences in order by writing a number in each space.

13 3 We chose a piece of meat.

14 1 We went out to get something for our dinner.

15 4 We paid the butcher for the meat.

16 5 We took the meat home to Mum.

17 2 We went to the butcher's shop.

Here are six questions followed by six answers. Choose a suitable answer to each question, and write it after the question.

18 Have you had your tea? .... *Yes, an hour ago.* ....

19 Where did you go for your holiday? .... *I went to Spain.* ....

20 When is the next bus? .... *At half-past ten.* ....

21 Are you going to wear your new dress?
    Yes, I want to look smart. ....

22 Did you get the flowers from the garden?
    No, there are none there. ....

23 Where is your pencil? .... *In my case.* ....

Answers:

Yes, I want to look smart.   At half-past ten.
In my case.   No, there are none there.
I went to Spain.   Yes, an hour ago.

Fill each space with a word from the list on the right.

24 The children ran .... *quickly* ....   quickly

25 The girl worked .... *neatly* ....   brightly

26 The lion snarled .... *fiercely* ....   fiercely

27 The sun shone .... *brightly* ....   softly

28 The snow fell .... *softly* ....   neatly

Write these sentences again, changing all the words in heavy type into the past tense (what has already happened).

29 The girls **play** in the garden.
        The girls played in the garden.

30 Tom **wears** his new shirt.
        Tom wore his new shirt.

31 Mum **gives** the baby a rattle.

Mum gave the baby a rattle.

32 The children **eat** their dinner.

The children ate their dinner.

33 The boys **sing** a carol.

The boys sang a carol.

The answers to the clues can be made from the letters in this word.

elephant

34	It is worn on your head	hat
35	A part of your foot	heel
36	Warmth	heat
37	A short sleep	nap
38	This is green and grows in a pod	pea
39	An animal you keep at home	pet
40	A busy insect	ant

Paper 3

Underline the right answers.

Early next morning Robin arose and set off, well pleased at the thought of meeting such a worthy foe. As he approached the riverside he saw, strolling along the bank, a huge and burly

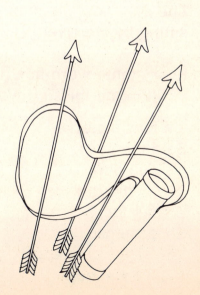

monk, dressed in a gown of brown cloth and with a girdle about his middle, but, unlike any other monk, he wore a knight's cap of steel upon his shaven crown. Also, there hung a sword by his side, and a large bag and bottle balanced it on the other side. Robin soon discovered the contents of the latter, for, sitting down, the knightly monk drew a good-sized pasty from the bag, and, first taking a long pull at the bottle, proceeded to dispatch the pie.

1   Whom did Robin meet near the river? (A monk, a foe, a knight)

2   What time of day was it? (Evening, morning, afternoon)

3   What was in the monk's bag? (A pasty, a bottle, a sword)

4   What was in the bottle? (Petrol, something to drink, a pasty)

5–6   What was the monk wearing? (A brown gown, a grey gown, a hat, a monk's cap, a steel cap)

7   "Strolling" means (rolling, walking slowly, running, walking fast)

8   The monk's hair was (short, long, burly, shaven)

9   The monk ate his meal (walking by the river, in a monastery, sitting by the river)

10–13   Every tenth word has been left out of the poem below. Try to fill in the missing words.

It's four o'clock
Said the cock
It's still dark
Said the lark
What's that?
Said the cat
I want to sleep
Said the sheep

A bad habit
Said the rabbit
Of course
Said the horse
Let's have a spree
Said the bee

14–18 Write this sentence again, putting in the capital letters.

my name is george watkins and i live in wigan.

My name is George Watkins and I live in Wigan.

Write either **a** or **an** in each space.

19–21 ...a... banana and ...an... apple and ...an... apricot

22–24 ...an... owl and ...a... robin and ...an... eagle

25–30 Some words are made of two words joined together, like **postcard**.
Can you sort out these mixed up words?

jellyball footberry goosefish carweed seapaper wallpet

goose berry   jelly fish   foot ball

car pet   sea weed   wall paper

Underline one word in the brackets which is connected with the words on the left.

31 apple plum peach   (jelly, lemon, drink, cream)
32 stand lie run   (match, seat, sit, hen)
33 kitten calf lamb   (dog, sheep, puppy, cat)
34 dull misty foggy   (bright, cloudy, weather, dry)
35 tiny short little   (size, smart, pretty, small)

Choose one word from the column on the right to complete each line.

36 As sharp as a ......needle......   honey

37 As quiet as a ......mouse......   needle

38 As cold as ......ice......   March hare

39 As sweet as ......honey......   mouse

40 As mad as a ......March hare......   ice

Paper 4

Underline the right answers.

Some words
about tails,
animals, fishes, birds,
from elephants to whales,
very nearly all ·
have tails, long or short,
straight, curly, fat, small,
monkeys, tortoises, tigers, cockatoos,
peacocks are vain, they like to spread
their dazzling tails out, but kangaroos
prefer to sit on theirs, lizard will shed
his bit by bit, then grow another.
Fox warms himself on chilly nights with his,
wrapped round sharp nose and head.

Leonard Clark

1   Which animal wraps his tail round himself to keep warm?
    (Peacock, kangaroo, <u>fox)</u>

2   Which animal is very proud of himself? (<u>Peacock,</u> elephant,
    fox)

3   Which animal sits on his tail? (<u>Kangaroo,</u> fox, cockatoo)

4   Which animal has a very pointed face? (Lizard, tiger, <u>fox)</u>

5   The (<u>lizard,</u> elephant, kangaroo) loses one tail and then
    grows another.

In the poem there are seven words which describe tails. Write
them below.

6   long   7   short   8   straight   9   curly

10   fat   11   small   12   dazzling

Some of these sentences make sense, and others do not. Put a tick for those which make sense, and a cross for the others.

13 The pretty fairy was very ugly. ....×
14 The little girl ran across the field. ....✓
15 The little boy drove the car through the town. ....×
16 Dad divided the cake into five quarters. ....×
17 The tree had fallen across the road. ....✓
18 Mum kissed the baby whom she hadn't seen for twenty years. ....×

What would these things contain? Underline the correct answer.

19 A sack   (insects, flowers, <u>potatoes</u>, hats)
20 A chest   (balls, <u>tea</u>, ships, bread)
21 A bottle   (fish, <u>milk</u>, butter, cake)
22 A trunk   (<u>clothes</u>, trees, plants, telephones)

Underline two words in each line which have something in common with the word on the left.

23–24 **bed**   <u>pillow</u>   clock   book   <u>sheet</u>   alarm

25–26 **book**   ball   <u>page</u>   door   cook   <u>cover</u>

27–28 **boat**   <u>sails</u>   car   run   <u>oars</u>   pen

29–30 **month**   <u>day</u>   mouth   food   <u>week</u>   weak

31–32 **town**   ocean   <u>shops</u>   whistle   <u>houses</u>   piano

Underline the word in each line which means the same as the word on the left.

33 **fell**   <u>dropped</u>   apple   rain   felt

34 **rush**   hour   bump   knock   <u>hurry</u>

35 **similar**   different   <u>same</u>   unkind   unlike

36 **beneath**   above   go   floor   <u>under</u>

37 **choose**   like   eat   <u>pick</u>   present

Make three long words out of these six short ones.

| table | card | ball | post | foot | cloth |

38 tablecloth   39 football   40 postcard

Paper 5

Underline the right answers.

Strange, strange, is the little old man
Who lives in the Grange.
Old, old, and they say that he keeps
A box full of gold.
Bowed, bowed, is his thin little back
Which once was so proud.
Soft, soft, are his steps as he climbs
The stairs to the loft.
Black, black, is the old shuttered house.
Does he sleep on a sack?
They say he does magic, that he can cast spells,
That he prowls round the garden listening for bells;
That he watches for strangers, hates every soul,
And peers with his dark eye through the keyhole.
I wonder, I wonder, as I lie in my bed,
Whether he sleeps with his hat on his head?
Is he really a magician with altar of stone
Or a lonely old gentleman left on his own?

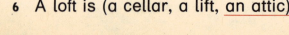

1-2 The old man is (small, tall, old, ill)

3-4 He is (fat, thin, strong, round-shouldered)

5 He walks upstairs (quietly, quickly, slowly, fast)

6 A loft is (a cellar, a lift, an attic)

7 What treasure do people say he has? (Jewels, <u>gold</u>, magic, spells)

8 People say he listens for (strangers, magic, <u>bells</u>)

9 I think he is probably (a magician, <u>a lonely old man</u>, a stranger)

Underline the word which rhymes with the word on the left.

10 **four**   hour   far   our   <u>pour</u>

11 **you**   bough   <u>flew</u>   how   though

12 **none**   <u>sun</u>   gone   lone   bone

13 **low**   cow   how   <u>mow</u>   through

14 **hair**   here   <u>care</u>   gear   fear

Underline one word in each line which has a similar meaning to the word on the left.

15 **modern**   <u>new</u>   old   ancient   times

16 **rapid**   fall   slow   <u>fast</u>   drop

17 **depart**   post   <u>go</u>   come   send

18 **smooth**   hilly   <u>flat</u>   high   bottom

19 **broad**   bent   broken   <u>wide</u>   long

Rewrite these sentences, putting in the capital letters.

20–24 i asked mr. brown if he would go to london on tuesday.

I asked Mr. Brown if he would go to London on Tuesday.

25–28 "my birthday is in october," said paul smith.

"My birthday is in October," said Paul Smith.

Underline the word which has an opposite meaning to the word on the left.

29	**right**	front	back	<u>left</u>	correct
30	**dark**	night	<u>light</u>	day	winter
31	**clean**	washed	ugly	clothes	<u>dirty</u>
32	**rich**	wealth	money	<u>poor</u>	ill
33	**safety**	<u>danger</u>	accident	crash	freedom
34	**here**	now	<u>there</u>	then	where

Underline the correct word in the brackets.

35 Daniel was very hungry, so he was (hopeful, depressed, <u>pleased,</u> enjoyed) when his mother gave him his tea.

36 They enjoyed the picnic so much that they (remembered, saw, watched, <u>forgot)</u> the time.

37 The old man usually walked slowly, so they were (<u>surprised,</u> reversed, quick, arrived) when he started to run.

38 The audience clapped after she had (repaired, <u>sung,</u> sighed, retired) the song.

39 The picture, which had been painted by a famous (actor, <u>artist,</u> statue, author) was presented to the art gallery.

40 The train is (departed, coming, <u>expected,</u> arriving) to arrive in half an hour.

Paper 6

In Mr. Reynolds' shop the shelves are full of tins, jars and packets of many kinds of food. In a special case there are packets of biscuits and small cakes. On the counter there are some boxes of crackers and decorations for cakes. There are always many people in Mr. Reynolds' shop because he is a very kind and polite man who never seems too busy to be helpful.

1–5 Underline the statements that are true.

The counter in the shop is bare.

Mr. Reynolds is too busy to be helpful.

<u>Mr. Reynolds helps his customers.</u>

<u>I think it is nearly Christmas time.</u>

Not many people go into Mr. Reynolds' shop.

<u>The biscuits and cakes are in a special case.</u>

<u>There is a lot of food in the shop.</u>

The crackers are on the shelf.

<u>"Polite" is the opposite of "rude".</u>

The words on the left are nouns. Underline another noun in each line.

6 **girl** pretty <u>book</u> go she busy

7 **house** it large red new <u>desk</u>

8 **paper** brown running <u>window</u> some our

9 **plates** <u>legs</u> dirty them broken their

10 **book** interesting long <u>cat</u> dull her

Underline the correct word in the brackets.

11 Boy is to girl as man is to (mother, father, <u>woman</u>)

12 Finger is to hand as toe is to (leg, <u>foot</u>, ankle)

13 Right is to left as black is to (<u>white</u>, coal, night)

14 Fish is to water as bird is to (nest, <u>air</u>, fly)

15 G is to letter as 7 is to (day, week, <u>number</u>)

Underline one word in each line which does not fit in with the others.

16 tree   plant   bush   flower   <u>bucket</u>

17 pink   <u>bright</u>   blue   yellow   green

18 <u>adult</u>   child   baby   boy   girl

19 several   <u>few</u>   many   lot   crowd

20 tall   large   <u>short</u>   big   long

21 chair   desk   table   <u>cushion</u>   sideboard

22–25 Write either **their** or **there** in each space.

There are their hats and their coats, over there .

Put one of these words in each of the spaces below.

   although   but   until   so   because

26 Marianne stayed at home because she had a cold.

27 The sea is quite warm so we can go swimming.

28 Mum is going out now but she will be back soon.

29 Gary wore his gloves although it was much warmer.

30 We will stay here until the bus comes.

31–34 Rewrite this sentence, putting in the capital letters.

on monday morning, matthew went to manchester.

On Monday morning, Matthew went to Manchester.

Put one of the words from the column on the right in each space.

35 The watchdog guarded the house.   curtains

36 The curtains looked colourful at the windows.   stars

16

37	The <u>children</u> are making a model boat.	teapot
38	The <u>birds</u> are building their nests.	children
39	The <u>teapot</u> was standing on the tray.	watchdog
40	The <u>stars</u> twinkled in the sky.	birds

Paper 7

Underline the right answers.

There was once a fat old pig called Flora, who was large and pink. She was kind and good, but she wasn't very clever. She had eleven piglets of whom she was extremely fond. She fed them and washed them and looked after their manners and she kissed them goodnight. The trouble was she simply couldn't count them.

Mrs. Tomkins, the farmer's wife, used to get so cross with her.

"Flora!" she would shriek out of her kitchen window, when she had found a piglet in her bath or in the ironing basket. "Flora! If you can't look after your own children I shall have to shut you all up in a shed and not let you in the farmyard at all!"

1 Mrs. Tomkins was cross because Flora couldn't
(feed the piglets, <u>count them,</u> wash them)

2–4 Flora was (<u>big,</u> lazy, clever, <u>pink,</u> cross, <u>kind</u>)

5–6 The piglets strayed into (the farm, <u>the ironing basket,</u> the shed, <u>the bath,</u> the kitchen window)

7 What was the trouble with Flora? (She didn't look after the piglets, she got cross with them, <u>she couldn't count</u>)

8 Mrs. Tomkins said she would (<u>shut them in the shed,</u> keep them in the farmyard, keep them in the kitchen)

Write **was** or **were** in the spaces.

9–10 Janice <u>was</u> in the garden, and her sisters <u>were</u> in the house.

11–12 Mrs. Tomkins <u>was</u> cross because Flora <u>was</u> unable to count the piglets.

13 The spaceships <u>were</u> getting closer all the time.

Underline one word which means the same as the first word.

14 **begin** finish first <u>start</u> end

15 **understood** <u>knew</u> forgot wondered read

16 **sick** thick <u>ill</u> well happy

Underline the correct word in the brackets.

17 The slam of a (wind, <u>door,</u> train, clock)
18 The chime of a (cork, drum, gun, <u>clock)</u>
19 The patter of (<u>feet,</u> a horn, a trumpet, a stream)
20 The ringing of (water, wings, <u>bells,</u> winds)
21 The dripping of (<u>water,</u> paper, feet, games)
22 The howling of (wings, <u>the wind,</u> a whip, wasps)
23 The beat of a (<u>drum,</u> bell, match, piano)

Rewrite the following sentences, putting capital letters in the right places.

24–26 sandra white lives in heswall.

Sandra White lives in Heswall.

27–29 aunt mary is going to ireland for her holiday.

Aunt Mary is going to Ireland for her holiday.

30–32 we are going to manchester on monday.

We are going to Manchester on Monday.

Write **a** or **an** in each of the spaces below.

33 *an* ugly monster   34 *a* pretty bird

35 *an* open door   36 *an* orange drink

37 *a* hot day   38 *an* apple tart

39 *an* even number   40 *an* old lady

Paper 8

Underline the right answers.

Many railway lines link London with other parts of the country. There are two main lines to Scotland: one goes up the east side of the country through York and Newcastle, and the other goes up the west side, passing through Crewe and Carlisle. If you are travelling to North Wales you leave the main line at Crewe. There are fast trains from Liverpool, Manchester and Sheffield to London and it is much easier to travel from north to south than it is to travel from east to west. There is a service from London to the west country which passes through Salisbury and Exeter. There is an excellent electric service between London and south-east England.

1–2 What kind of service is there between London and south-east England? (Slow, <u>electric</u>, <u>excellent</u>, could be better, poor)

3 If you are travelling to North Wales, where do you leave the main line? (Sheffield, <u>Crewe</u>, Carlisle)

4–5 If you are travelling to Scotland on the east side of the country, which of these towns would you pass through? (Crewe, York, Salisbury, Manchester, Carlisle, Newcastle)

6–7 If you are travelling to Scotland on the west side of the country, which of these towns would you pass through? (Crewe, Exeter, Salisbury, Carlisle, Newcastle)

8 Which is it easier to do? (Travel from east to west, travel from north to south)

Use the words **and**, **but** or **because** to fill the spaces.

9 I like macaroni ...but... my brother likes spaghetti best.

10 I went to the baths ..because.. I wanted to swim.

11 I am short ...and... my brother is short too.

12 I asked her to come ...but... she wanted to go home.

13 The sky was blue ...and... the sun was shining.

Choose one of the words below to fit each space.

error   cautious   herd   adult

14 group of cattle ......herd......   **15** careful ..cautious..

16 grown-up ...adult...   **17** mistake ...error...

Here are six jumbled words. Find out what they are, and then put one in each space in the story below.

lacape   rifay   ncipre   peels   esert   ncipress

18 Years passed, and still the princess lay in a deep ...sleep... .

19 One day a ..prince.. came riding by, and he wondered

20 what was behind the tall ...trees.... An old man told him

21 that a wicked ...fairy... had cast a spell on everyone in

22 the ...palace... and that the spell wouldn't be broken until

23 the .princess. was rescued by a handsome prince.

Underline the correct word in the brackets.

24 Where (as, has) he put the cards?

25 She has (eat, eaten, ate) her tea.

26 Ricky has (broken, broke, broked) the window.

27 He (one, beat, won) the swimming race.

28 (Its, It's) not on the table.

Look at these pairs of words. If they are alike in meaning, write **A**.
If they are opposite, write **O**.

29 first   last   O

30 go   stop   O

31 lost   found   O

32 open   shut   O

33 allow   let   A

34 never   always   O

35 terror   fear   A

36 feeble   weak   A

Write these shortened words in full.

37 Mon.   Monday

38 Mr.   Mister

39 Dr.   Doctor

40 Oct.   October

Paper 9

Underline the right answers.

Take a trolley, push it round,
Castor sugar? Get a pound.
There's the cocoa, take a tin.
Here's a loaf but it's cut thin.
There's another, that will do.
Now we'll find some jam for you.
Choose a jar. Yes, strawberry

Will suit your Dad and also me.
A tin of fish, a bag of rice,
That cream-filled cake looks very nice.
We must have soap and toothpaste too,
This green shampoo will do for you.

Supermarket by Barbara Ireson

1 We are in a (station, <u>supermarket,</u> school)

2 Do we like thin bread? (Yes, I do not know, <u>no)</u>

3 Castor sugar is (<u>fine sugar,</u> brown sugar, cube sugar, coarse sugar)

4–6 Who likes strawberry jam? (<u>The mother, the father, the child,</u> no one)

7 Why do we need a trolley? (To put our cases in, to put our baskets in, <u>to put the food in)</u>

8 We got a bag of (shampoo, <u>rice,</u> soap, a loaf)

9 We bought (3, 9, <u>10,</u> 12) things.

10–14 Underline the correct words in the brackets.

I went (<u>to,</u> too, two) the sea, and my (to, too, <u>two)</u> friends went (to, <u>too,</u> two). The other (to, too, <u>two)</u> went (<u>to,</u> too, two) the zoo.

Fill in these spaces. The words on the left should give you a clue.

15 brave He was awarded a medal for his <u>bravery</u>.

16 strong Samson was famous for his <u>strength</u>.

17 proud Our classroom is tidy. We take great <u>pride</u> in it.

18 hungry Many people in India suffer from <u>hunger</u>.

19 wide "Do you know the <u>width</u> of this material?"

22

Underline the right word in the brackets.

20 A desk never has (legs, arms, a top, a lid).
21 A tree never has (roots, branches, leaves, tails).
22 A bird never has (feathers, a dress, wings, a nest).
23 A rose never has (petals, thorns, pins, buds).
24 A horse never has a (shoe, hat, saddle, mane).

Put a tick at the end of the lines which have the same meaning.

25–26 Tanya got into hot water. ....✓..............
       Tanya washed her face. ....
       Tanya got into trouble. ....✓..............

27–28 Dad put the cat into a bag. ....
       Dad let the cat out of the bag. ....✓..............
       Dad did not keep the secret. ....✓..............

29–30 Mark had the lion's share. ....✓..............
       Mark ate the lion's dinner. ....
       Mark had the largest part. ....✓..............

31–32 Mum said it was a storm in a teacup. ....✓..............
       Mum said it was a fuss over nothing. ....✓..............
       Mum spilt some tea in the cup. ....

On the left of the page are the names of eight different kinds of people. On the right are some of the things these people would use in their jobs. Write the names of the tools beside the person who would use them.

33	carpenter	nails and hammer	plough and tractor
34	tailor	needle and thread	scissors and comb
35	farmer	plough and tractor	needle and thread
36	teacher	blackboard and chalk	brush and paints
37	hairdresser	scissors and comb	saddle and bridle
38	sailor	compass and anchor	compass and anchor
39	artist	brush and paints	nails and hammer
40	jockey	saddle and bridle	blackboard and chalk

Paper 10

Underline the right answers.

First, fill the kettle with water and switch it on. Warm the teapot, and put in a teaspoonful of tea for each person, and one extra. This is called one for the pot! When the kettle has boiled, pour hot water into the teapot and put on the teacosy. Leave it to brew for a few minutes. Now you can get out cups, saucers, teaspoons, milk and sugar.

1 First you (fill the kettle, fill the teapot, boil the kettle)

2 How many teaspoons of tea per person should you put in?
(1, 2, 3, 4)

3 What is the name of the extra spoonful?
(Extra, kettle, one for the pot, teaspoon)

4 Why do you need a teacosy? (To look pretty,
to keep the tea hot, to stop the tea from spilling)

5 When should you pour hot water into the teapot?
(When the kettle has boiled, when you have put on the
teacosy, when you have found the cups)

6–7 What do some people put in their tea?
(Sugar, saucers, milk, a teacosy)

8 What are saucers for?
(To catch spills, to look pretty, to keep the tea hot)

9 What would be a good title for this passage?
(A party, Making coffee, How a kettle works,
How to make a pot of tea)

Give the group name for the things named on each line.

10 Liverpool Chester Manchester Reading   *towns*

11 hammer chisel saw screwdriver   *tools*

12 Cheshire Dorset Devon Norfolk   *counties*

13 elm oak ash beech   *trees*

14 hamster cat cow sheep   *animals*

15 England France Wales Spain   *countries*

Underline the word which has the same meaning as the first word.

16 **aid**   act   hinder   <u>help</u>   said

17 **drop**   rain   prod   bounce   <u>fall</u>

18 **stern**   <u>strict</u>   sad   glad   ugly

19 **quick**   quack   <u>fast</u>   slow   speed

20 **several**   few   even   <u>some</u>   ever

21 **enjoy**   hate   <u>like</u>   suffer   food

Put these words in the order in which you would find them in a dictionary.

peach   honey   kipper   ice-cream   jelly   jam

22 (1) *honey*   23 (2) *ice-cream*   24 (3) *jam*

25 (4) *jelly*   26 (5) *kipper*   27 (6) *peach*

In each space, write **were** or **where**.

28 We *were* going for a ride.

29 I don't know *where* you put it.

30–31 After we *were* told the book was lost, John said he knew *where* to look for it.

32–33 This is *where* we *were* lighting the fire.

25

Make seven new, long words by pairing these short ones.

34 space *ship* woman

35 sheep *dog* market

36 police *woman* apple

37 super *market* ship

38 pine *apple* fruit

39 grape *fruit* rover

40 land *rover* dog

Paper 11

Underline the right answers.

Grey as a mouse,
Big as a house,
Nose like a snake,
I make the earth shake,
As I tramp through the grass;
Trees crack as I pass,
With horns in my mouth
I walk in the South,
Flapping big ears,
Beyond count of years
I stump round and round
Never lie on the ground
Not even to die.

From *Oliphaunt* by J. R. R. Tolkien

1 What am I? (A dark house, a big tree, a hippo, <u>an elephant</u>)

2 "Nose like a snake" means (snakes like climbing up my nose, <u>a trunk that can twist round to pick things up,</u> my nose is poisonous)

3 "Horns in my mouth" means (in a circus I play a horn, my horns are my teeth, <u>my horns are my tusks</u>)

4 "Beyond count of years" means (I am very young, <u>I am very old,</u> no one has tried to count)

5 "To stump around" means (a round tree stump, I have short legs, <u>I walk clumsily</u>)

6 "Trees crack as I pass" means (<u>I crash into them,</u> the trees bend, the leaves fall off the trees)

7 (An earthquake, a thunderstorm, <u>my heaviness</u>) causes the earth to shake.

Underline the words which should start with a capital letter.

8–13 Mr. Scott visited <u>edinburgh</u>, <u>glasgow</u> and <u>perth</u> each <u>friday</u>. <u>he</u> then travelled on the overnight train to <u>london</u>.

Underline the "doing" words.

14 I <u>walk</u> in the South.

15 He <u>drove</u> the bus into the garage.

16 Dave <u>hated</u> the new school.

17–18 As Karen <u>watched</u> through the window, Concorde <u>landed</u>.

Make words ending in **ing** from the words at the beginning of each line, and use them to fill in the spaces.

19 swim   David is <u>swimming</u> in the sea.

20 cut   Mum is <u>cutting</u> the Christmas cake.

21 save   Marian is ...saving... her pocket money.

22 hit   Nicholas is ...hitting... the ball.

23 laugh   The baby is ...laughing.. with her mother.

24 live   They are ...living... in a caravan.

Choose the most suitable ending from the list below to finish each sentence.

> she had hurt herself
> cycled on
> he was late
> it was raining
> it was a windy day
> she was thirsty

25 The leaves fell from the trees because ...it was a windy day...

26 The little girl was crying because ...she had hurt herself...

27 Jane put up her umbrella because ...it was raining...

28 Mum made a pot of tea as ...she was thirsty...

29 Peter hurried to school but ...he was late...

30 Simon mended his bicycle and ...cycled on...

Write either **their** or **there** in each of the spaces below.

31   The children went out to play with ...their... friends.

32   ...There... isn't going to be any rain today.

33–34 ...Their... shoes are over ...there... on the floor.

Underline the correct word in the brackets.

35   It was a very happy (seen, <u>scene</u>).

36   I have never (<u>seen</u>, scene) so many people there.

37　The (bough, bow) of the tree had broken off.

38　The man gave the Queen a graceful (bough, bow).

39　There was a big (hole, whole) in the ground.

40　The (hole, whole) school went to see the play.

Paper 12

Underline the right answers.

　　If you want to have a pet, you should think carefully about how you will have to look after it. Animals have feelings, just as we do, and it is cruel to have a pet when you don't have time or money to look after it. A dog, for instance, needs lots of meat, which is not cheap. Also, you must take it for walks every day. A cat needs less food, and can take itself out, but you must still feed it twice a day and look after it.

　　Animals in cages – rabbits, guinea pigs, birds, mice – need cleaning out! So think before you buy a pet.

　1　Dogs eat (meat, cake, yogurt)

　2　Which animals in the passage need the most food?
　　(Cats, guinea pigs, dogs)

3–4　Dogs need (meat, cats, walks, pets)

5–8　(Dogs, cats, rabbits, guinea pigs, birds, mice) live in cages.

　9　What would be a good title for this passage?
　　(The rabbit, Pet problems, Cage birds)

The following sentences are not in the right order. Read them through carefully, and then put numbers to show the order in which they should come.

10   *3*   The doctor said he must stay in bed.
11   *4*   A few days later he was able to get up.
12   *1*   Jonathan did not feel at all well.
13   *2*   His mother sent for the doctor.

14   *3*   The train drew in to the station.
15   *5*   They all went home.
16   *2*   They waited for the train to arrive.
17   *1*   Tamsin and Ian went to the station.
18   *4*   Mummy and Daddy got off the train.

19–24 Fill in the blanks.

The spaceship was coming nearer and nearer, and Dart *tried* to see the alien beings inside. But there didn't *seem* to be any windows. Then landing wheels came down *with* a clunk, and the spaceship landed on the planet's *surface*. When it had come to a standstill, a metal *door* slid open, and there they were! The space people *had* arrived!

Underline one word in each line which does not fit in with the other words.

25 rain   sun   puddle   shower   dampness

26 look   glance   see   flew   watch

27 table   chair   stool   seat   bench

28 night   darkness evening dusk   morning

29 sea   ocean   hill   lake   river

30

30–32 Fill in the missing words.

Jane helped her mother to set the .....table..... She put out the .....knives...., forks and spoons, and then the plates, cups and .....saucers.....

33–37 Fill in the blanks.

It was a clear September night and the moon .....shone..... so brightly down through the water that he could .....not..... sleep even though he shut his eyes as tight .....as..... possible. At last he came up to the top .....and..... sat upon a little point of rock. He looked .....up..... at the broad, yellow moon.

Below are three questions and three answers. Choose a suitable answer to each question and write it in the space by the question.

38 Where is your coat?   It is hanging in the cupboard

39 Where are you going?   To get some sweets

40 Why are you wearing gloves?   Because it is cold

Answers: Because it is cold.
It is hanging in the cupboard.
To get some sweets.

Paper 13

Underline the right answers.

John and Michael took their pennies and chose their favourite horses. They stood watching the merry-go-round, and two horses seemed more beautiful than the others. Their names, printed in curly letters on their necks, were For Fun and Spit Fire. They had scarlet saddles and their backs were painted in green and blue and cherry-red, with diamonds of scarlet and scrolls of gold. Their mouths were open, showing white teeth, and red tongues lolled out. Their gold eyes flashed, and their heads were thrown back in the speed of their running. They looked magnificent. The boys rode on these two all afternoon until their money was spent. It was grand to career on these galloping horses, with their red nostrils and their carved golden manes.

1–4 Which parts of the horses were completely red? (Their backs, mouths, eyes, heads, manes, nostrils, saddles, diamonds, tongues)

5 Why did the boys stop riding? (They felt ill, they went too fast, they had no more money, they were tired)

6 To "career" is (to move very quickly, to do something, to do a job)

7 Nostrils are (part of a horse's harness, part of his mane, part of his nose)

8–10 The horses had gold (names, scrolls, diamonds, teeth, eyes, manes, heads)

Put an apostrophe in the right place.

11 The man's hair
12 The boy's hand
13 My sister's foot
14 The baby's toy
15 The lady's basket

Choose one of these words to fit each space.

voyage   remedy   summit   annual   fragment

16 Every year ...annual...

17 Journey by sea ...voyage...

18 A piece broken off something fragment

32

19 A cure ...remedy...

20 The top ...summit...

In each line there is a word which rhymes with the first word.
Underline this word.

21 **cow**   few   to   low   how   so

22 **two**   tow   do   go   sew   know

23 **sign**   none   bun   bin   sin   line

24 **knew**   few   knife   know   low   bow

25 **height**   hit   weight   write   bait   wait

Underline a word in the brackets which is connected with the
words at the beginning of the line.

26 boat liner yacht   (sea, ruler, pond, ship)
27 run play skip   (quiet, noisy, jump, rope)
28 minute day second   (hour, clock, first, March)
29 chisel axe saw   (view, hammer, ox, hand)
30 butter cheese jam   (dish, plate, bread, board)

Put these words into the past tense (what has already happened).

31 go ...went...   32 sing ...sang...

33 am ...was...   34 fight ...fought...

35 buy ...bought...   36 come ...came...

Below are four words which can be used to describe colours.
Write the describing word in the space before each colour.

bottle   coal   rose   nut

37 ...rose... pink   38 ...nut... brown

39 ...bottle... green   40 ...coal... black

Paper 14

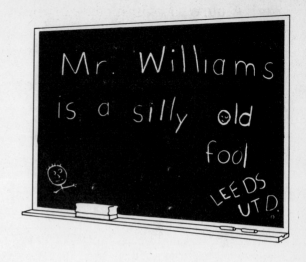

Mr. Williams
is a silly old
fool
LEEDS
UT.D.

Underline the right answers.

"Quick!" said Mark. "Hide! He's coming, I can hear his footsteps."

The two boys looked wildly round the room for somewhere to hide. The desks were too small, the teacher's store cupboard was locked–and those footsteps were getting closer all the time. Miserably, the two boys crouched behind the teacher's table, but they knew they were not very well hidden. All Mark could think about was what he had written on the blackboard: "Mr. Williams is a silly old fool."

1 There were (1, 2, 3, 4) boys.

2 They were in a (house, flat, shop, classroom)

3 Why did they look round "wildly"? Because (they felt ill, they were afraid of being caught, they were lost)

4 What had they done wrong? (Hidden behind a table, written on the blackboard, run away)

5 Who is coming down the corridor?
(The headmaster, Mark, Mr. Williams, the caretaker)

6 What do you think will happen next? (Mr. Williams will be pleased with them, Mr. Williams will be cross with them, they will go home)

The five vowels are **a, e, i, o** and **u**, and there is always at least one vowel in every word. Put the missing vowels into these words.

7   There are 24 of these in a day.   h **o u** r s

8   Bees make this in their hives.   h **o** n **e** y

9   Very unkind and hurtful.   c r **u e** l

10 Not difficult.   **e a** s y

11 Where you go to catch a train.   s t **a** t **i o** n

Underline the correct word in the brackets.

12 Fast is to quick as halt is to (go, come, <u>stop)</u>
13 Sun is to day as moon is to (<u>night,</u> dark, winter)
14 This is to that as here is to (hat, where, <u>there)</u>
15 Boy is to foot as dog is to (tail, <u>paw,</u> fin)
16 Mouth is to taste as nose is to (hear, look, <u>smell)</u>

Choose the most suitable word from those on the right to put in each space.

17 The ducks quacked ....**loudly**....   fiercely

18 Ian ran ....**quickly**....   loudly

19 The fire burned ....**fiercely**....   quickly

20 The soldier stood ....**stiffly**....   stiffly

Rewrite the following lines, putting in question marks, inverted commas, capital letters, commas and full stops.

21–24   Where is it asked the boy

"Where is it?" asked the boy.

25–28   Give out the books said the teacher

"Give out the books," said the teacher.

29–34 Have you seen my hat called wendy going to the door

"Have you seen my hat?" called Wendy, going to the door.

Each of these words has two meanings. Can you match each word to each pair of sentences?

till   flat   leaves   tramp   chips   ground

35 Joe and his dad lived in a } **flat**
The landscape looked very }

36 Ginger which is crushed into powder is } **ground** ginger.
Sam slipped from the tree and fell to the }

37 Don't cross the road } **till** { I tell you.
The cashier's } { showed a big bill.

38 We'll go for a long } **tramp** { through the fields.
The poor old } { had no warm clothes.

39 The sculptor } **chips** { away at the stone.
Let's have fish and } { for lunch.

40 The teacher } **leaves** { at the end of term.
The fallen } { blocked up the gutter.

Paper 15

Underline the right answers.

The next day was quite a different day. Instead of being hot and sunny, it was cold and misty. Pooh didn't mind for himself, but when he thought of all the honey the bees wouldn't be making, a cold and misty day always made him feel sorry for them. He said so to Piglet when Piglet came to fetch him, and Piglet said that he wasn't thinking of that so much, but of how cold and miserable it would be being lost all day and night on the top of the Forest. But when he and Pooh had got to Rabbit's house, Rabbit said it was just the day for them, because Tigger always bounced on ahead of everybody, and as soon as he got out of sight, they would hurry away in the other direction, and he would never see them again.

From *The house at Pooh Corner* by A. A. Milne

1–2 The next day was (hot, wet, sunny, cold, raining, misty)

3–4 The day before it was (hot, wet, sunny, cold, raining, misty)

5 Pooh was sorry for (Tigger, Piglet, the bees, himself)

6 Piglet was thinking about (the bees, Pooh, being lost in the forest)

7 Pooh and Piglet went to (Rabbit's house, Tigger's house, Pooh's house)

8 (Pooh, Tigger, Piglet) always went ahead.

9 When Tigger got out of sight, Pooh and Piglet (followed him, went the other way, stood still)

10 (Tigger, the bees, Rabbit, Piglet) came to fetch Pooh.

11 (Piglet, Rabbit, Pooh, Tigger) wasn't thinking of himself.

In each line underline the word which is the baby of the word on the left.

12 **dog**	kitten	doe	hen	puppy	hog
13 **lion**	vixen	cub	cygnet	tiger	lioness
14 **pig**	sow	calf	piglet	hind	buck
15 **duck**	drake	fledgling	chicken	doe	duckling
16 **frog**	fish	tadpole	toad	eel	insect

Fill each space with a phrase from the list.

later on   near   help   everyone
many times   travelling very quickly   decide

17 Again and again .... *many times* ....

18 Going like the wind .... *travelling very quickly* ....

19 By and by .... *later on* ....

20 Make up your mind .... *decide* ....

21 One and all .... *everyone* ....

22 Lend a hand .... *help* ....

23 Close at hand .... *near* ....

Underline the word which best describes the first word in each line.

24 **station**   flower   sea   just   <u>busy</u>

25 **pencil**   wet   <u>sharp</u>   sleepy   dull

26 **hands**   ten   happy   <u>clean</u>   first

27 **June**   <u>sunny</u>   foggy   dark   frosty

28 **hair**   sticky   sweet   quiet   <u>straight</u>

Underline the correct word in the brackets.

29–30 Sam makes (<u>good</u>, well) cakes. He sews (good, <u>well</u>).

31–32 John James acted (good, <u>well</u>), and we thought the film
        was (<u>good</u>, well)

33–34 How (good, <u>well</u>) you can paint. I wish I could paint (<u>good</u>,
        well) pictures.

35–36 The team played (good, <u>well</u>) and made a (<u>good</u>, well)
        score.

Once upon a time, outside the British Museum, there lay two stone lions. They were very big. One was a very kind, contented lion, and lay still all day long. But the other lion licked a man coming out of the door of the museum. He was surprised. "What do you think I am?" said the man, "an ice-cream?"

Four of the statements below are correct. Draw a line under these.

37–40   The lions lay still all day.

One lion licked a man going into the museum.

The man was amazed.

The man looked like an ice-cream.

A man coming out of the museum was licked by the lion.

The lion was surprised.

The lions were made of stone.

The man spoke to the lion.

Paper 16

Underline the right answers.

They fetched the Christmas tree from the market, and Sarah couldn't wait to start decorating it. Mum got the box of decorations down from the loft, and brushed the cobwebs from it. First they took out the fairy lights, and plugged them in. They worked, so Mum wound them round the tree. Next came tinsel, silver and red, and coloured glass balls. Sarah was very fond of them. They were the same ones every year, unless one was broken. When the tree was finished, Sarah stood on a chair and carefully put the fairy on top.

1 They bought the tree from a (shop, <u>market,</u> lorry)

2 Sarah felt (<u>excited,</u> bored, frightened)

3 Why were there cobwebs on the box? (Because there were too many spiders, <u>because it had been in the loft all year,</u> because Sarah's Mum did not hoover)

4 The lights were worked by (gas, <u>electricity,</u> wind)

5 What was silver and red? (The glass balls, <u>the tinsel,</u> the tree, the fairy)

6 How did Sarah feel about the glass balls?
   (<u>She liked them,</u> she hated them, they made her laugh)

7 Christmas trees are put up (every week, every day, <u>every year)</u>

8 What was the last decoration to go up?
   (The tinsel, the lights, <u>the fairy,</u> the balls)

9 Why did Sarah stand on a chair? (Because there was a mouse on the floor, to reach the top of the cupboard, <u>because she couldn't reach the top of the tree)</u>

Underline the word which has an opposite meaning to the word on the left.

10 **fancy**   <u>plain</u>   cake   funny   dress

11 **large**   size   high   wide   <u>small</u>

12 **sorry**   sad   upset   <u>glad</u>   happy

13 **none**   never   <u>all</u>   some   nobody

14 **noise**   nose   din   row   <u>quietness</u>

Underline the correct word in the brackets.

15 Steven (run, <u>ran</u>) quickly to the field.
16 We (<u>passed</u>, past) the church.
17 Michael (break, <u>broke</u>, broken) the cup.
18 Daddy (<u>did</u>, done) the puzzle.
19 The time is half (passed, <u>past</u>) two.

The answers to the clues all begin with the letters **pl**.

20 To put in position   pl <u>a c e</u>

21 It grows in the garden   pl <u>a n t</u>

22 Not fancy   pl <u>a i n</u>

23 A scheme   pl <u>a n</u>

24 We put our food on it   pl <u>a t e</u>

Write these shortened words in full.

25 N.E. <u>north east</u>   26 P.T.O. <u>please turn over</u>

27 Rd. <u>road</u>   28 Ist <u>first</u>

29 S.W. <u>south west</u>   30 St. <u>street (or saint)</u>

Rewrite the following sentences, making the words in heavy type plural.

31–32 The **knife is** sharp.

        <u>The knives are sharp.</u>

33–34 The **woman** picked up the **child**.

        <u>The women picked up the children.</u>

35–36 The **leaf was** yellow.

        <u>The leaves were yellow.</u>

37–40 Your **foot is** too big for **this slipper**.

        <u>Your feet are too big for these slippers.</u>

Paper 17

Underline the right answers.

The following morning we gathered our stores together, packed all we could into bags, and fixed these across the backs of the animals. The fowls were coaxed into the tent with some handfuls of corn, and then we put them safely into two hampers.

The stores that we could not carry were packed into the tent, and casks and chests piled round as a protection.

We formed a strange procession. My wife and Fritz led the way. Then came the laden cow and ass. Jack, with the monkey on his shoulder, drove the goats. Ernest managed the sheep, and I came last, while Turk and Bill seemed happy in guarding us all.

We travelled slowly across the bridge, and when any animals were tempted to stray, to eat the rich grass, the dogs brought them back to an orderly line.

1   The stores were put (in a chest, on the backs of animals, in hampers)

2–3 (Turk, my wife, Bill, Fritz) led the way.

4   (Fritz, Ernest, Jack, Turk) looked after the sheep.

5   (Fritz, Ernest, Jack, Turk) took an animal on his shoulder.

6   What was given to the fowls? (Corn, meat, hampers)

7   The dogs (chased the fowls, managed the sheep, kept the animals from straying)

8–9 (My wife, a cow, Turk, Jack, an ass) carried bags.

10 Jack (managed the sheep, led the way, drove the goats)

Rewrite these sentences, changing the words in heavy type to the past tense (what has already happened).

11–12 The children **go** to school and **see** their teacher.

The children went to school and saw their teacher.

13–14 Lisa **sits** in the garden in a shady place she **knows**.

Lisa sat in the garden in a shady place she knew.

15–21 In the following passage every tenth word has been left out. Try to fill in the right words.

Once upon a time there was a horse whose ....name.... was Scrappy. He was a rag and bone man's ....horse.... He often met his friend Blackie who was a ....dog.... Now Scrappy didn't want to be a rag and ....bone.... man's horse, but he wanted to be a racehorse ....and.... win the Derby. And Blackie, who had rather short ....legs...., wanted to be able to run as fast as ....a.... greyhound.

Underline one word in each line which does not fit in with the others.

22 <u>road</u>   snow   hail   ice   frost
23 fast   <u>car</u>   quick   speedy   rapid
24 cotton   <u>shirt</u>   wool   nylon   silk
25 duck   hen   <u>lamb</u>   chicken   goose
26 doctor   builder   plumber   <u>garden</u>   policeman

Put **a** or **an** in each space.

27–28 ....a.... bow and ....an.... arrow

29–30 ....an.... acorn from ....an.... oak tree

31–32 ....a.... kite and ....a.... skateboard

33–34 ....an.... egg and ....a.... sausage

35–36 ....a.... stick and ....an.... umbrella

What am I?

37 I am usually round, and people boil water in me.
I am a <u>kettle</u>

38 I am round and I bounce and children play games with me.
I am a <u>ball</u>

39 I am a small animal. My coat is soft but I have sharp claws.
I purr when I am happy.
I am a <u>cat</u>

40 I am a small animal with a bushy tail. I collect nuts for my
store.
I am a <u>squirrel</u>

Paper 18

Read the following passage and then write **True** at the end of
each line which is correct, and **Not true** against any which are
wrong.

When she was only three years old, Maria Celli loved to
play the violin. By the time she was five, she was having violin
lessons from a master who thought she was extremely clever.
Her parents were very proud of Maria, and they loved to hear
her play. When she was eighteen she gave her first concert in
London.

1 Maria started to play the piano when she was
five.   <u>Not true</u>

2   Maria was taught the violin by a master.   True

3   Her parents loved to hear her play.   True

4   Her parents were very proud of her.   True

5   She gave her first concert in London.   True

6   She gave her first concert when she was five.   Not true

7   Her parents taught her to play.   Not true

8   Maria didn't like playing the violin.   Not true

9   Her master thought that she was very clever.   True

Underline the correct word in the brackets.

10   The tramping of (clocks, <u>feet</u>, wood)

11   The braying of (people, ducks, <u>donkeys</u>)

12   The barking of a (door, cat, <u>dog</u>)

13   The ticking of a (cloth, <u>clock</u>, cock)

14   The tooting of a (<u>horn</u>, tiger, gun)

15   The boiling of a (bull, <u>kettle</u>, horse)

From the list below find the opposite of these words.

    thin   above   depth   down

16   height   depth   17   below   above

18   up   down   19   fat   thin

See if you can fill in the spaces.
Clue: each word ends in **ful**.

20   Someone who is always helping people is
    a   helpful   person.

21   Someone who hopes for something is being   hopeful

22 The king had a great deal of power. He was
a ....*powerful*.... king.

Write the days of the week in alphabetical order.

Monday Tuesday Wednesday Thursday Friday Saturday
Sunday

23 1st is ....*Friday*....

24 2nd is ....*Monday*....

25 3rd is ....*Saturday*....

26 4th is ....*Sunday*....

27 5th is ....*Thursday*....

28 6th is ....*Tuesday*....

29 7th is *Wednesday*

30–33 Put a line under any word which can be given an opposite
meaning by putting **un** before it.

<u>popular</u>   thick   <u>washed</u>   <u>tidy</u>   glad   <u>fair</u>   cold

34–40 In each of the spaces below write one of the following
words.

goalkeeper   playing   evening   excited
match   team   captain

The children were very ....*excited*.... as there was to be a
football ....*match*.... against another school. They picked
their ....*team*.... and then they practised every ....*evening*.....
Tony, their ....*captain*...., was very pleased with the way they
were ....*playing*...., and especially with John who was a very
good *goalkeeper* .

Paper 19

Underline the right answers.

Today's a day I've not enjoyed.
Today's a day I've been employed
In sorting out and tidying:
In rummaging then emptying
Into the rubbish bin
All sorts of things
Not fit for use.
Some old tin toys with broken springs:
A fat clown puppet with tangled strings:
A fire engine whose wheels got stuck
All had to go—I'm not sure why.
(For order's sake I'm told)
Oh dear—it really makes me want to cry,
For worse, much worse than all of this—
Today my wellies were thrown out.

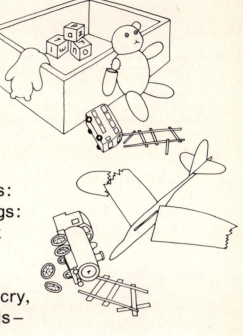

1   Why was I unhappy? (I had to empty the rubbish bin, I had to throw away all my toys, <u>I had to throw out broken toys</u>)

2   "I've been employed" means (I've gone out to work, <u>I've been busy doing something,</u> I've been enjoying)

3–4   What things did I have to throw out? (My wellies, a bat, <u>tin toys with broken springs,</u> a doll's house, <u>a fire engine</u>)

5   Why does a puppet have strings? (So it can be tied up, <u>to move its head, arms and legs,</u> to pack it away)

6   The worst thing that happened was (I had not been well, I had to clear out my toys, <u>my boots had been thrown away</u>)

A farmer, a fisherman, a gardener, a cook, a teacher, a doctor and a garage man were talking about their jobs.

7   If she was talking about a hospital, medicines and nurses she was a   doctor   ....

8 If he was talking about pastry, an oven and recipes he was a .... cook

9 If he was talking about boats, nets and herring he was a .... fisherman

10 He was talking about cars, petrol and pumps so he was a .... garage man

11 A .... gardener .... would talk about spades, plants and soil.

12 A .... teacher .... would talk about chalk, books and children.

13 Crops, animals and tractors would be talked about by a .... farmer

Underline the right answers.

14 A snail lives in a (stable, form, house, <u>shell</u>)
15 A bee lives in a (<u>hive,</u> kennel, nest, den)
16 A pig lives in a (waggon, kennel, <u>sty,</u> lodge)
17 A lion lives in a (purse, <u>den,</u> cell, trap)
18 A horse lives in a (<u>stable,</u> tent, class, camp)

Underline the two words in each line which are nouns.

19–20 short   <u>socks</u>   silly   loose   <u>money</u>
21–22 hard   thin   <u>leader</u>   <u>lesson</u>   more
23–24 rough   <u>sea</u>   swimming   blue   <u>sand</u>
25–26 <u>slipper</u>   they   warm   furry   <u>bed</u>
27–28 small   brown   <u>horse</u>   <u>glove</u>   busy

Choose one of these verbs to fill in each space.

dripped   splashed   poured   spread   stirred   mashed

29 The children, who were playing in the bath, ... splashed .... the water on the floor.

30 Mum .... mashed .... the potatoes for dinner.

31   I .....spread..... the butter on the bread.

32   Dad .....poured..... the milk over our cornflakes.

33   Julie .....stirred..... the Christmas pudding.

34   The water .....dripped..... slowly from the tap.

Antony likes outdoor games; he is very popular with the other
boys, and he is untidy and noisy.
Brian is artistic and he likes making things. He is neat and quiet.

Underline the sentences that are correct.

35–40   Antony likes playing football.

Brian's books are not very tidy.

Brian likes painting.

Brian likes craft lessons.

Antony is a quiet, tidy boy.

The other boys like Antony.

Antony would rather do carpentry than play cricket.

Antony is often told he must not make so much noise.

Antony would rather play cricket than stay indoors.

Paper 20

Underline the right answers.

Poor prisoner in a cage,
I understand your rage
And why you loudly roar
Walking that stony floor.

Your forest eyes are sad
As wearily you pad
A few yards up and down,
A king without a crown.

Up and down all day,
A wild beast for display,
Or lying in the heat
With sawdust, smells and meat.

Remembering how you chased
Your jungle prey, and raced,
Leaping upon their backs
Along the grassy tracks.

But you are here instead,
Better, perhaps, be dead
Than locked in this dark den;
Forgive us, lion, then,
Who did not ever choose
Our circuses and zoos.

Leonard Clark

1 Who is the prisoner? (A man, a lion, a king)

2 "You pad" means (you put stuffing into,
you walk up and down, you pant)

3 "Forest eyes" are (green eyes, brown eyes, wooden eyes,
eyes used to seeing things in a forest)

4 "Jungle prey" is (something you ask for in the jungle,
stories about wild animals, an animal you kill in the jungle)

5 Does the person who wrote the poem like circuses and
zoos? (Yes, I don't know, no, sometimes)

6 Why might it be better for the lion to be dead?
(It must be terrible for a lion to be kept in a cage, it was
getting old, it might kill someone in the zoo)

7 Why do they call him a "king without a crown"?
(They put a crown on him in the circus, his mane looks like a crown, <u>the lion is known as the king of animals</u>)

Write one of these words in each of the spaces below.
but   although   than   and   if

8 He tried to open the door <u>although</u> he had seen the man lock it.

9 I would rather have tea <u>than</u> coffee.

10 Joe wanted to buy some sweets <u>but</u> he hadn't enough money.

11 I shall go for a swim <u>if</u> it is warm enough.

12 The girls are going camping <u>and</u> the boys want to go too.

Make words ending in **ing** from the words at the beginning of the lines, and write them in the spaces.

13 come   The girls are <u>coming</u> along the road.

14 dig   Kevin is <u>digging</u> in the garden.

15 swim   The boys are <u>swimming</u> across to the island.

16 leave   They are <u>leaving</u> the hotel.

17 put   Mum is <u>putting</u> on her new dress.

18 drive   The farmer is <u>driving</u> his tractor.

Underline the correct word in the brackets.

19 Eye is to see as ear is to (watch, smell, <u>hear</u>)
20 Back is to front as left is to (behind, side, <u>right</u>)
21 Top is to bottom as up is to (<u>down,</u> below, above)
22 North is to south as west is to (north, <u>east,</u> south)
23 High is to tall as fast is to (train, <u>quick,</u> slow)
24 Cold is to hot as miserable is to (bad, ill, <u>happy</u>)

Choose a word from the column on the right to complete each line.

25 The _lions_ prowled the forest.   tree

26 The _goldfish_ swam round the bowl.   goldfish

27 The _tree_ was old and bent.   harvest

28 The _monkey_ sprang from branch to branch.   frog

29 The _worm_ wriggled through the soil.   worm

30 The _frog_ croaked loudly.   lions

31 The _harvest_ is gathered in.   monkey

Write the following lines in a shortened form, using the apostrophe.

Example: The hand of the lady
          The lady's hand

32 The pencil of Ravi _Ravi's pencil_

33 The shoes of my father _My father's shoes_

34 The toys of the children _The children's toys_

35 The paw of the dog _The dog's paw_

36 The jeans of the girl _The girl's jeans_

Every tenth word has been left out of this rhyme.
See if you can fill them in.

37–40 One little Indian boy making a canoe
       Another came _to_ help him and then there were two.
       Two little _Indian_ boys climbing up a tree
       They spied another and _then_ there were three
       Three little Indian boys playing on _the_ shore
       They called another one and then there were four.

Paper 21

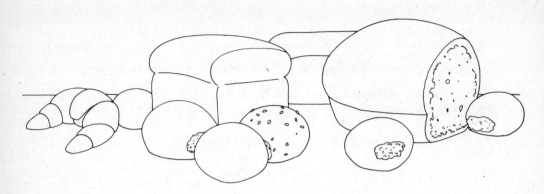

Underline the right answers.

Making bread

Sift the flour and the salt into a large mixing bowl. Add the fat and rub into the mixture. Make a hollow in the centre of the ingredients. Measure the water very carefully into another bowl. The water should be hand-hot (in other words you should be able to hold a finger in it with comfort). Stir in the sugar and then sprinkle the yeast on to it. Set aside in a warm place for about ten minutes. Then pour the yeast mixture quickly into the centre of the flour. Use both your hands to mix it all to a dough. Then turn it out on to a board and knead the dough for about ten minutes.

1–2 What two things do you put into the water?
  (Salt, <u>sugar, yeast,</u> flour)

3–4 What two things do you put in with the flour?
  (<u>Salt,</u> sugar, <u>fat,</u> yeast)

5 Which one of these things must be sprinkled on to a mixture? (Salt, sugar, <u>yeast,</u> fat)

6–7 You are told to do two things for ten minutes. They are (mix with your hands, leave the flour and salt aside, <u>knead the dough, set the yeast mixture aside</u>)

8 The water you use should be (boiling, <u>hand-hot,</u> warm, cold)

9–12 In the following passage four words are spelled wrongly. Put a line under them and write them correctly below.

They had a wonderful tea. Lots of hot scones and <u>rasberry</u> jam, very <u>stickey</u> gingerbread, buns with raisins and <u>currents</u> in them, and, best of all, a big, round chocolate cake with a special filling made by Dawn's mother. Rover, the dog, was given dog biscuits spread with meat paste. "Wuff," said Rover, and thumped his <u>tale</u> hard.

raspberry   sticky   currants   tail

Complete the following.

13 Sh! You must be very qu i e t so that they can't hear you.

14 We received the post c a r d you sent us.

15 I bel i e ve you are telling the truth.

16 The g u a r d waved his flag, and the train started.

17 A f o r t n i g h t is two weeks.

Underline the word which doesn't fit in with the others.

18 rabbit   mole   weasel   <u>owl</u>   hare
19 <u>together</u>   tonight   tomorrow   yesterday   today
20 uncle   sister   <u>Sally</u>   aunt   brother
21 cinema   shop   house   <u>horse</u>   hotel
22 cross   <u>pleased</u>   angry   furious   annoyed
23 skates   toboggan   skis   <u>ship</u>   sledge

Put the commas in these sentences.

24 Diane is making a blouse, a skirt and a dress.

25–26 Steven bought some potatoes, carrots, cabbages and onions.

27–29 At school we study English, mathematics, history, geography and many other subjects.

Fill each space with a phrase from the list.

soon	not well	sleepy	badly treated
make a new start			

30 Ill used .... *badly treated*

31 Turn over a new leaf .... *make a new start*

32 Out of sorts .... *not well*

33 In a short time .... *soon*

34 Heavy eyed .... *sleepy*

Put the following words in the order in which you would find them in a dictionary.

sunflower   tulip   violet   thistle   rose   snowdrop

35 (1) .... *rose*   36 (2) .... *snowdrop*

37 (3) .... *sunflower*   38 (4) .... *thistle*

39 (5) .... *tulip*   40 (6) .... *violet*

Paper 22

Underline the right answers.

I'd like to be a barber and learn to shave and clip,
Calling out, "Next please," and pocketing my tip.
All day long you'd hear my scissors going "snip, snip, snip,"
I'd lather people's faces and their noses I would grip
While I shaved most carefully along the upper lip.
But I wouldn't be a barber if . . .
      The razor was to slip
         Would you?

The barber by C. J. Dennis

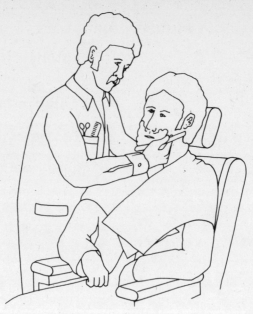

1. "Pocketing my tip" means (the tip of my comb sticks out of my pocket, <u>extra money given by customers goes in my pocket,</u> I put hair cuttings in my pocket)

2. To "lather" is (to ladle, <u>to put soap on,</u> to launder)

3–4. A barber's job is to (<u>cut hair,</u> work in an office, <u>shave men,</u> work in a laundry)

5. He used scissors for (shaving men's faces, cutting pockets, <u>cutting hair)</u>

6. "I wouldn't be a barber if the razor was to slip" means (barbers never let razors slip, if I let the razor slip I wouldn't be a barber, <u>I would get into a lot of trouble)</u>

Underline the word which means the same as the word on the left.

7	**nation**	ribbon	food	strong	<u>country</u>
8	**pointed**	jewel	<u>sharp</u>	badge	watch
9	**circle**	square	peg	<u>round</u>	oblong
10	**busy**	lazy	hard	soft	<u>active</u>

Underline the correct word in the brackets.

11   Ian had never (see, <u>seen,</u> saw) such a big boat before.

12–13   (Has, <u>As)</u> it is snowing, John (<u>has,</u> as) put his boots on.

14   I have (<u>given,</u> gave, give) the present to my father.

15   Caroline is the girl (which, what, <u>who)</u> plays with me.

Make the words in heavy type into their opposites by adding **un** at the beginning.

16   Sean was a very **popular** ....*unpopular*.... boy.

17   Let's **cover** ....*uncover*.... the mess.

18   This coat is **suitable** ....*unsuitable*.... to wear in the rain.

19   I may be **able** ....*unable*.... to help you.

The following sentences are not in the right order. Read them carefully, and then put numbers to show the order in which they should come.

20   *3* David said, "No."

21   *5* He finished writing his story.

22   *2* He asked David if he could borrow his pen.

23   *1* While Jason was writing a story his pen broke.

24   *4* Jason said he would have to use a pencil.

25   *3* A policeman came up and asked what had happened.

26   *4* An ambulance arrived.

27   *2* The cyclist lay on the road.

28   *1* The motorist knocked down a cyclist.

Rewrite these sentences, changing them into the plural (more than one).

29–30 The girl was laughing.

.......................The girls were laughing.......................

31 The thief escaped from jail.

...............The thieves escaped from jail...............

32–33 The glass is full.

.......................The glasses are full.......................

Choose a suitable word from the column on the right of the page, and write it in the space.

34 The ...policeman... blew his whistle.   bath

35 The .....doctor..... gave me some medicine.   clock

36 The .....clock..... was five minutes fast.   parcel

37 The .....winter..... had been a very cold one.   moon

38 The .....bath..... was full of water.   winter

39 The .....parcel..... was tied with string.   doctor

40 The .....moon..... shone very brightly.   policeman

Paper 23

Underline the right answers.

It is very difficult to think of anything nicer to share between six children than an empty house. Number Four had, of course, the same number of rooms as the other houses in the Lane, the

two bedrooms upstairs, the front room, the kitchen, and the scullery sticking out at the back, which was almost a room each, and that is how they divided up the house. The front room was given to Marge and Millie to share, and the other rooms divided naturally. Freda had the kitchen, because she liked cooking things. Dickie had the scullery, because he was messy with his carpentering. Sally and Dave each had a bedroom. Of course, the children were not really allowed into Number Four, which belonged to the Council. It had never been said that they were not to go in; it was just known that they could not, and that was where the especial charm of the house lay, because they had found their own way in, and nobody knew anything about it.

From *The children of Primrose Lane* by Noel Streatfeild

1 There were (2, 3, 4, 5, 6) children.

2 There were (3, 4, 5, 6) rooms.

3 There were (3, 4, 5, 6) girls.

4–5 (Sally, Marge, Dave, Millie) shared a room.

6 (Sally, Dave, Dickie, Freda) was messy.

7 (Sally, Freda, Marge, Millie) liked cooking.

8 The house was owned by (Sally, the children, no one, the Council)

9 The house was number (3, <u>4</u>, 5, 6)

10 There were (1, <u>2</u>, 3, 4) bedrooms.

11–12 Which children had a bedroom? (<u>Sally</u>, Marge, Millie, <u>Dave</u>)

13–14 They liked being in the house because (they were told to go there, <u>they knew they could not go there</u>, they were locked in the house, <u>they had found their own way in</u>)

Underline all the adjectives in the passage below. An adjective is a word which describes a noun.

15–23 The <u>tall</u> man, who had a <u>kind</u> face, walked into the <u>busy</u> town. He went into a <u>large</u> shop, and bought a <u>wooden</u> bat and a <u>red</u> ball. They were put into a <u>brown paper</u> bag, which he took home for his <u>young</u> son.

24–29 Fill in the gaps.

Whenever I walk in a London street,
I'm ever ...<u>so</u>... careful to watch my feet;
And I keep in ...<u>the</u>... squares,
And the masses of bears,
Who wait at ...<u>the</u>... corners all ready to eat
The sillies who tread ...<u>on</u>... the lines of the street,
Go back to their ...<u>lairs</u>... ,
And I say to them "Bears,
Just look how ...<u>I'm</u>... walking in all the squares!"

If you want to keep leaves for winter decorations the best way is to iron them! Pick the leaves on a dry day, and then press them on both sides with a fairly hot iron. The iron must not be too hot or it will scorch the leaves. Put an old cloth on your ironing-board to protect it.

30–33 Put a line under any of the following sentences which are correct.

Put a cloth on the ironing-board to protect the leaves.

60

The best way to preserve leaves is to iron them.

The iron must be very hot.

The leaves must be scorched.

Iron the leaves on both sides.

Use a fairly hot iron.

Pick the leaves on a hot day.

Protect the ironing-board with a cloth.

Form an adjective linked with the word on the left.

34   interest   It was an .....interesting..... programme.

35   boredom   Ian thought the laundrette was .....boring.....

36   truth   Is this a .....truthful..... story?

37   pain   Gary's cut knee was very .....painful.....

38   darkness   Tricia peered into the .....dark..... room.

39   taste   That was a .....tasty..... meal.

40   wool   Mum is knitting a .....woolly..... jumper.

Paper 24

Underline the right answers.

When everything else is silent
in the dead of winter,
there are still some birds singing.
Perched on a bare branch, the mistlethrush
braves the snowstorm with a wild song,

bold robin pipes up cheerily every day;
on dull afternoons, a couple of starlings
whistle and chuckle on rooftops,
the nervous wren, skulking in hedgerows,
surprises with a loud voice.
Loveliest of all, when mornings are calm,
a few notes of pure silver drop from the skies
where a single skylark hovers in sunlight,
as far away as springtime
and all its choirs of sweet singers.

Leonard Clark

1 Which bird hides in the hedges? (Cuckoo, thrush, wren)

2 Which bird flies high in the sky? (Wren, skylark, robin, thrush)

3 Which bird is bold and comes near people? (Wren, skylark, robin)

4 "The dead of winter" means (all the things that have died in winter, everything that is dead, mid-winter)

5 The skylark's song is like (drops of pure silver, the morning, spring-time)

6–7 The wren's voice is (nervous, lovely, loud), and the (robin, thrush, wren) has a wild song.

8–12 Which birds do we hear singing in the winter? (Cuckoo, skylark, thrush, tit, starling, nightingale, robin, wren)

Put one of these words in each space.

for   inside   after   out   through   over

13 Look ....after.... your toys, then they won't get broken.

14 Look ....inside.... the cupboard. Your book may be there.

15 Look ....over.... the wall. The ball may be in the next garden.

16 Look ....out....... of the window. Can you see them?

17 Look .....through.... the magnifying glass. The ant looks larger.

18 Look ....for....... the pen you lost. You are very careless.

19–26 Read the story, and then choose words which are the opposites of the words in heavy type. Take the words from this list. You will not need them all, so choose the most suitable ones to write in the spaces.

horrible   boy   never   woman   holiday   angry
closed   man   rude   girl   worst   uncomfortable

After the holiday, the **man** (.....woman....) went back to the travel agent, feeling very **pleased** (.....angry.....), and said to the **woman** (.....man.....) at the counter, "My holiday in Spain was the **best** (.....worst.....) I have ever had. The hotel was very **comfortable** (..uncomfortable..), the food was **delicious** (.....horrible.....), and the staff were very **polite** (.....rude.....). I will **always** (.....never.....) go to Spain for my holidays in the future."

Underline the word which is the feminine of the word on the left.

27 **wizard**   fairy   woman   <u>witch</u>   warlock

28 **actor**   player   <u>actress</u>   lady   author

29 **husband**   mother   father   <u>wife</u>   aunt

30 **uncle**   nephew   <u>aunt</u>   niece   sister

31 **he**   her   him   them   <u>she</u>

Underline the words in each line which rhyme.

32–34 <u>crane</u>   <u>pain</u>   pan   crate   trial   <u>train</u>

35–37 back   <u>ache</u>   poke   <u>flake</u>   <u>take</u>   lock

38–40 <u>ghost</u>   closed   <u>post</u>   lost   <u>toast</u>   baked

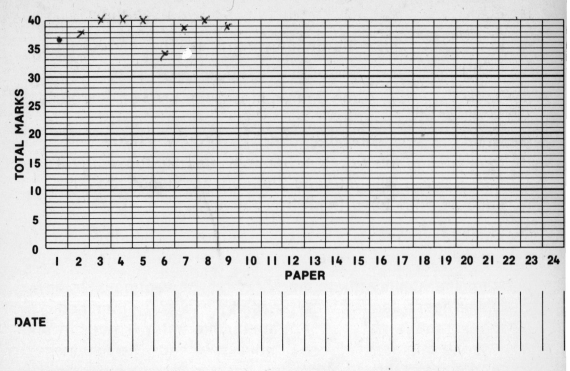

DATE

Thomas Nelson and Sons Ltd
Nelson House   Mayfield Road
Walton-on-Thames   Surrey KT12 5PL   UK

51 York Place
Edinburgh EH1 3JD   UK

© **J M Bond 1970, 1983, 1987**
First published by Thomas Nelson and Sons Ltd 1970
Second edition 1983
Revised edition 1987

Pupil's Book ISBN 0-17-424463-0
              NPN 9 8
Answer Book ISBN 0-17-424464-9
              NPN 9 8 7 6

By the same author
Introductory, First, Second, Third and Fourth Year
Assessment Papers in Mathematics

Introductory, First, Third and Fourth Year Assessment
Papers in English

First, Second, Third and Fourth Year Assessment
Papers in Reasoning

Filmset in Nelson Teaching Alphabet
by Mould Type Foundry Ltd
Leyland   Preston   England

Printed in England
by Ebenezer Baylis & Son Ltd
The Trinity Press   Worcester and London

Poems and extracts reproduced by kind permission of

Angus & Robertson (UK) Ltd: **The barber** from *A book
for kids* by C J Dennis (Paper 22)
Dobson Books Ltd: **Tails** (Paper 4), **Lion** (Paper 20) and
Songs (Paper 24) from *Four seasons* by Leonard Clark
George Allen & Unwin: **Oliphaunt** from *Adventures of
Tom Bombadil* by J R R Tolkien (Paper 11)
The Hamlyn Publishing Group Ltd: **Supermarket** by
Barbara Ireson (Paper 9)

A M Heath & Co Ltd: Extract from *The children of
Primrose Lane* by Noel Streatfeild (Paper 23)
Mr C R Milne and Methuen, London: Extract from *The
house at Pooh Corner* by A A Milne (Paper 15)

The publishers have made every attempt to trace
copyright holders of reprinted material, and apologise
for any errors or omissions.